AF492300

The Day Everything Changed.

Index.

<u>Preface.</u>

This collection of poetry was inspired by an event which changed a few things in my life. On one hand in confirmed a few things personally to me, on the other hand it gave me confidence to step forward with what I wanted to do in my life.
The day was August 14th 2021, and although that might not seem like a long time ago, things on this day made things in my personal life slot together, like a hand slipping inside a silk glove.

This collection of poetry does indeed follow on from my collection of work "My Loving Astraller." Which was published January 2022, the collection of poem in that book shows the elements of an astral being who has haunted me for a few years and still to this day continues to haunt me.

However these collection "The Day Everything Changed." Is based round the inspiration and confirmation of things that happened on that summers day 2021, a day when I learnt my sanity is not to be questioned, nor my gifts as a medium, I should trust in the universe let alone my own gut feeling.
The poems you will read in this book are personal to this event and this day, they were written in the space of 48 hours when I was filled with a sense of truly knowing, truly believing. Although the poems are personal they refer to multiple things that happened as well as emotions in day to day life.

5
To the core I now know I'm not insane, I maybe
different, but I rather be quirky and myself than lost in a
crowd of faces.

<u>Personal Messages.</u>

To Nicoletta,
Thank you for inviting me to your event in Dalston, it was a wonderful and insightful evening. Hopefully these poems reflect the elements of inspiration the evening brought to me let alone give inside to what I've been dealing with.
You deserves every success, you are truly an inspirational person and I honour you for that.
So to you, a personal thank you.

**

To My Friend,
Thank you for coming with me to London, thank you for supporting me when I had that panic attack in London and thank you for telling me I'm not crazy.
To have shared and witnessed that moment, telling me that it was indeed real, and for you to keep me from questioning it even now, I do honestly mean thank you when I say it.
I honestly don't know how I would of handled that evening on my own, so thank you for going with me and being there with me.

**

7

To My Parents,
thank you for having my mini me for that weekend. I
know its a rarity and I know it is
hard work, I'm glad he was as good as gold for you and
that you all had fun.
Thank you for everything, love you so much.

**

To My Son,
Your my mini me, and I love you so very much. Thank
you for being the way you are, for bringing the smiles
when I've cried, for all the hugs and kisses and
laughter, you are so very bright my little monster.
I'm proud of you and I wish I could give you so much
more, whatever you do in your life, please follow your
dreams, follow your heart.

**

To You And Your Dog,
You will know who you are, should you ever read this.
Just know that I thank you for that smile you showed
me, thank you for that confirmation, love warmth and
kindness, those feelings I've always felt from your
energy.
Your fur baby is truly as beautiful as you are, and in that
moment that our eyes connected, that moment time
stood still, that time is truly etched upon my mind.
So to you with my heart opened wide, thank you.

To Myself,
I'm not insane, I'm normal for me.
I know it is real, however unreal it may seem.
Yet those closest to me have observed it as well, and now we both know it is real.
I will not slip into insanity, I will not question my own gut feeling or my own senses.

**

To You, The Reader,
Thank you for taking the time to read this book, a book written and edited in the space of forty-eighty hours. A book inspired by an event in my personal life on a summers day in 2021.
And now we come to the poems, so enjoy and remember I'm not insane, just inspired.
So on to the poems!

<u>Stagnant Years.</u>

It was like time had stood still
it slipped, drifting further out of reach.
Perhaps it was mostly hidden from view
just out of sight
for I know at that time, I was blind.
For the sands of life will never return
once they are lost, they become a memory.

I knew I was alone
yet I was still numb to life in all its splendour
for in my truest sense, deep within my heart
I knew I had learnt to be numb
I knew I was numb to life then
but still, unaware of time fading away.

Back then, those four years of nothing
I stood stagnant, as the waters of life carried on
I watched life from outside, yet never my own
I created that numbness out of pain,
perhaps it was my defence to hide?
To exist in a haze, to be numb and fade away
yet I still knew I wasn't living
even now, I know it was no life at all
I was just existing
it was a haze where days blurred together.

Nothing ever changed, why should it?

If I, myself, will not change.

Four long hazy years that slipped away
now that I'm awake to life
I regret time slipping away
it is a cold harsh truth, ageing,
it is a bitter pill that I've now swallowed
I realise now, I'll soon be thirty
then it will be another year
time doesn't stand still, only I stood still
that's when one's perspective of life changes.

For it is now that I've learnt some harsh truths
it is not the waters of life that are stagnant
it is never life itself or time that stands still
it is us, what we, ourselves, do
we make ourselves stagnant.

Life is a gift, time is fleeting
slipping away, drifting further into memory
life is to be lived within the present
for the present will become the past
like the blinking of our eyes
and the future, well that remains unseen.

So to those stagnant years that passed me by
well, I don't remember them fully
they are just the flashes of my eyelashes
yet four long years of a stagnant life
stagnation of living, that's a long time.
Four long years of being lost, forgotten in time

now just memories of nothing.

<u>Beginning Again.</u>

I've lived, I've explored
I've visited cities, towns and villages alike
some known, some hidden gems
I've gone to castles, museums, galleries
even to those events of oddities.

I've dressed scruffy,
I've also dressed in the vanity of glamour,
yet all those elements of what I was
well, they have long since become a silent life.

I'm a mother now
but that is no excuse
I know that something's I can't do
but it's not stopped me and my son from exploring
a few visits here, a few visits there.

Four years of limited adventure
was four years of limited imagination
not just for me but for my son as well.
Why did I become like this?
Why did I allow it to be like this?

Life was on hold time was fading
sunlight would rise and fall
moonlight would do the same,
yet adventures had become lost

somehow abandoned and forgotten.

It wasn't that I hadn't tried to do anything

but they were few and far between
just glimpses of existence
but not as life should be
at least not as I had first planned it to be.

It is unfair of me to have put life on hold
for life was silent for me
why should life be silent for my son?
I was the reason for that change
it's my fault that I took so long
changing what was needed for our future.

So, the time has begun again
learning to walk a path of our true adventure
life in its fullest, just like a newborn baby again
but what is life for me?

Life is what I made it
so I'm grabbing it tightly and living fully
not just for me but for my son
I will help those that I can
for charity is good for the heart, mind and soul.

But in truth, charity starts at home
but my charity at home?
Well, that is to begin again
to learn to live fully again
to enjoy the adventures to their fullest.

Panic.

Tomorrow's the day
we will attend that event
we've been looking forward to it
but our nerves are shockingly active.

It's just a poetry book launch,
it's being held in London.
To all senses of the word, it should be fun
but still, I need to prepare.

Why do I feel I need to do these face masks?
Why do I have to fully tog up and look the part?
I guess it's cause I want to be my best
yet why?
Why do I want to look my best?

Looking my best is stressful
weeks of preparing, weeks of planning
my head filled with ideas
thoughts of what-ifs and would or could be
the constant inner battle of self-judgement
not fitting in, not being good enough
being the one standing out like a sore thumb.

Panic has truly set in
I need to be ready, but I just need to breathe
everything is packed ready for the drive

Bartie is ready to stay with his grandparents
yet I'm still preparing mentally for that drive
let alone the evening ahead.

What if I can't find parking nearby?
What if someone takes offence to how I look?
What if we get stuck in traffic?
What if we are late?

What if...
these two words have become cruel
haunting me within my mind
like the curses of bitter tongued judgements
they roll around and around inside my head
it's a never-ending, crippling mentality
why can't they just be silent?

Yet there I am, in London now
stood at the parking meter
my mind's blank, panic always at its worst;
Why now do I have to have this curse rise?
I thought I had to pay, panic consumed me
I knew I didn't have the coins to feed the meter.

But a friendly voice from a window above
"Excuse me, love, you don't need to pay, it's free to
park here after one-thirty."
Thank you to that man from the window
I must've looked like an idiot
either that or out of place
I know I was totally out of my depth
utterly lost.

Panic like that makes me stress far worse
I'm that ratter bitch that hates herself
I'm not a nice person when I'm like that

it's a dark element of my demonic side
yet inside, when this is going on
I'm screaming to calm down,
screaming for help.

<u>Poor In Fur!</u>

Stoke Newington Road,
is a very odd place indeed.
Elements of all, walk here
those neon clothes of mortals
rushing in to fill seedy clubs.
The goths, vampires and wolves alike
rub shoulders together
all seeking safety in the shadows.

But some are poor
you get the homeless in any city or town
but oddly, on this street
these people who dress to be struggling
are something else completely.

They've no shame in coming to your table
"Can you spare a little change?"
a dirty hand outstretched
yet the nails are well manicured.

In many ways, I can understand their struggles
but their skin is often too clean
especially for those true rough sleepers.
The police stand idle by a vegan takeaway
they don't seem to bother by the fakes
they don't seem to notice the scammers

so waiting staff have to fend off these rogues
hoping to keep dating couples peace
let alone safe from falling into a trap.

17

Oh it is hard for the homeless
if they truly are rough sleepers
but they who fake it, that is cruel and low.
Being truly homeless is soul-crushing
your clothes would be dirty, your hair knotted
and your skin, well it would be rotting.
Your sleepless nights, harder in the cold months
the joy of a hot meal, a warm bed
that's a blessing
let alone for a true rough sleeper
a true blessing
well that would be a comfort
especially knowing they are safe.

If only those fakes could learn to act better
this scam they perform may well be entertaining
yet there they strut
playing their parts of fake homeless lifestyles.

Sometimes these fakes will stop you
"Oh love, firstly you look lovely!"
They often begin with that line,
to some unsuspecting women.
"I don't mean to be any trouble, but could you spare
some change!"
they continue,
often reaching out to touch her hand of rings.

Little do they know this woman's unwell
her mild panic attack,
getting worse by the second.
She needs to be alone

she does not need this right now
"Sorry, I've no change to give!"
Her reply was almost a squeak of fear
weak, as she walked away.

Then there at the bar
I sit and observe some more of this street
when one such fakery catches my eye.
A woman, in a lilac fur jacket
it's well kept
but its been doctored to look dirty
the wearer however claims to be homeless,
so where did the jacket come from?
It fits too well to be given to her
so yet alone fake,
yet alone, scam artists poorly achieve.

Lord save me from these acts of trickery
they are so bad, they would make Loki blush
con artists at their worst
these fakes give a whole new meaning
to that old special saying
Fake it, till you make it.

<u>Vegan Rock Bar.</u>

A rock bar with a modern twist
vegan food in grunge fashion
yet so typical of London's stylish look,
yet this vegan rock bar
holds a strange element.

How alien it may be to some
a vegan rock bar,
though these elements of style
they are unmistakable
yet still, it's all in keeping with the location.

To the bar, I walk with my friend in toe
that sticky floor beneath my witchy heels
all I can see is that clear screen,
protection they call it,
it's just a sheet of clear PVC
but it is that reminder of the year
that's been and gone before us all
this is now how all places are
such a topsy turvy scene to the world.

Still, a smile of a barman is welcoming enough.
"Two coffees, please, latte if you'd be so kind."
the words flutter from my tongue like silk

he just smiles, nodding in respect.
"Where will you be sitting, I'll bring them over."
He politely says in response
while tapping the screen of a digital till.

I point across the room
to a booth seat near the door
its dark grey leather seat of welcomed comfort.
"Great, that's £4.90 please"
the barmen once again replies
as I tap the black box of a cardholder
paying for an evening buzz to keep me going.

How little I think of that plastic payments
its become so normal
a sad excuse for currency in modern life.
Paper money seems almost like a toy
it's rarely seen at all now.
I wonder if money is indeed ever real?
Money these days is just numbers on a screen
like the childish numbers of a calculator
often spelling out the word 9009.

I take my seat, I'm safe here
no more panic attacks
I survived the drive through London
the nightmare I truly dread,
but this is my first night out in years
still, I remember why I don't go out any more.

It isn't long before the lattes arrive at the table
still, I'm surveying my surroundings
that oat milk in the latte

it's smooth across my tongue
yet, my eyes are focused upon the wall
to that neon light of a skull hanging there.

21

Yes indeed, this is a vegan rock bar
elements of biker gothic fusions
but truly I can say
this is a haven for us creatures of shadow.

<u>Flutter-bys And Sparkles.</u>

Step carefully down those metal stairs
that echoing sound of every heeled footstep
flutters in my stomach, crashing against each other
my nerves are bad again, but it will be fine,
I'm safe, just take a deep breath
I'm here in my element.

Yet here I go being early as ever
as always making a scene, shinning as who I trying am
I arrive with command of my own self-will
I won't lose my inner control
nor will that voice tell me over and over again
"I'm watching, I'm here!"

Man be silent!
I don't need to know your near
just be SILENT!
Let me have this night to shine as myself.

Then I realise I'm at the last step
turning and seeing the host of this event
her energy of bright joy from creativity
a fellow creature of shadow
surrounded by darkness and sparkles
elements of her inner self.

She who commands her own fate
she is a witch, a goth, a vampire
she's a poetess, and she is in her own element.

In many ways I envy her
she can be herself
like we should all do,
yet chips of bitterness from the past
they twist within us
lurking there deep within our nervous wrecks
they beat us down, controlling us.

I greet her and hug her for good luck
words of congratulations and good fortune
for there she stands in gothic elegance
for you, my dear friend, are in your element
tonight is your night, you're queen here.

So wear your sparkling crown with pride
don't worry if the lights no longer work
the lights of the ceiling are enough
for they cast the sparkles even more.

So say bye-bye to those flutter-bys
ignore the no shows, those who let you down
for tonight is truly your night
be the poetry queen that you are!

<u>Voice From Behind.</u>

I know that voice!
That male voice of silver-tongued charm
but I dare not look round,
I just know it's him.

Still, I need to be sure
so I carefully look out the corner of my eye
towards my friend beside me
thankfully he too has heard that voice
my eyes need to be fixed in front of me
so I'll look to my friend commanding the stage.

Yet, I see her eyes flashing around
looking out across the room before her
to me, then behind, then to me again.

Surely she does not know?
I've told her none of this situation,
none of this insanity that follows me,
he who shall remain nameless
he who I admire, yet fear
I do not even know him physically
nor do I know if this connection is even real.

No!

I can't think like that
I'm here to enjoy an evening of poetry
I'm here to support my friends work!
Still, I hear that voice again from behind me
it can not truly be his voice, can it?

Once again I glance to my friend beside me
I guess partly in hope of safety
but I'm not blind, nor foolish
my friend looks round to the mirror behind me
his eyes going wide, quickly looking away.

All my friend gives is a nod of his head
it is then I know for sure
that voice that I can here behind me
belongs to who I suspect
that voice of sliver-tongued charm,
my devil of the astral realms.

But he does not stay here long
it's clear he doesn't want to get noticed
nor does he want to steal the show,
this isn't his night, like it isn't my night
this isn't his event, or my event
but I hear his voice no more
so I guess that's it, his gone.

Yet, it's such a fleeting feeling
that knowledge of him being so close
but I'll never truly know myself,
if it was truly him
for I'm too much of a coward to look behind me
maybe, just maybe, our paths will meet again.

<u>Black Feathers, Blue Feathers.</u>

Black under bust corset,
is it satin, or is it silk?
That black dress of 1950's style
nothing less than classical elegance
it harnesses your inner gothic glow.

Yet, wings across your shoulders
shades of black feathers and electric blue
wings of power, wings of strength,
maybe even wings of protection.

Who am I kidding?
You've an army behind you, and before you.
Your strong, and command the scene well
these surroundings are your comfort zone.

<u>Time To Go.</u>

We've been here an hour
we've listened and observed,
but my gut is telling me it's time to go,
so can we please leave?

A nod of your head, a deep breath of relief
I say my goodbyes, my final congratulations
then walk back up those stairs, out into the street
only to be kissed by that breath of fresh air
that blessing of cool summer night air,
its somehow relaxing.

We walk to my car, parked nearby
it's not far to walk, but my feet ache
I want my flat shoes rather than these heels
don't get me wrong, I love my heels,
but I'm sick of them now.

A simple turn of the key in ignition
plug in the phone, set up the sat-nav
then away we drive, along that robotic route,
but something's odd
this turning isn't right, nor is this route
oh well, lets see where we end up.

<u>Something's Wrong.</u>

No, really, something's gone wrong
the sat-nav's being weird,
I need to stop and sort it out
honestly, I need to park up
this routes all wrong.

Let's take this turning,
oh wait, I know this place
how do I know this place?
Why do I recognise this street?

No, wait, not here, not now, I'm not ready!
I can sense him, that energy of him
that sliver-tongued devil,
that beauty of spiritual elegance
he is here, he is home
and he is indeed very near to me!
I can sense him, just as much as he can sense me!

I'm too close, I shouldn't be here
then again, maybe I should?
This is what I've been waiting for
this is what I asked the universe to provide me
a sign, just one sign,

that this connection was indeed truly real
so maybe I'm exactly where I should be.
But I can't stay here long,
that would seem weird to on lookers
so let me sort this sat-nav out.

29

Oh my, that energy is every so strong now
but why now? Why here?
A flash inside my mind
that telepathic image
then in an instant I look up to the path nearby
at first your not there.

No, wait, just another moment,
you are there, oh my!
You are there,
looking at me, as I look at you.

<u>Chanced Encounter.</u>

I sat in the drivers seat of my car
that blanket of night covering the sky above
with just the haze of the city's glow.
I was bathed in orange of that street light
but there I am, still sat in my car
fumbling hopelessly with my sat-nav.

That sudden image in my mind
you walking your even sweet dog
the image was so real I was forced to look up
thinking I was finally losing my mind.

I gazed out of that window into the silent street
its almost like a ghost town here
yet I know the city is still ablaze with life
but its twenty to eleven
that's an early hour in London's breath of life
but in this corner of the city
it's quiet like a ghost town..

Still, I look across to the path beside my car
part of me is hoping that the image within my mind
is indeed real,
but another part of me is hoping it is not.

Nothing seems to come forward alone the path
so I go back to my sat-nav,
hoping I can sort the route out
but my eyes notice movement nearby

that softness of chocolate fur
I can not help it but my eyes dart to that direction.

There, not a hundred yards away from me
is your four legged fur baby
out for an evening walk, with you.

At first I just saw him, physical and real
I could not help but say the words
"Oh Bobby dog!"
then my eyes followed his lead to your hand
and the shame of what I said washed over me.

I know my eyes widened in surprise
surely my voice was equally in shock
I know I was heard by you.

You had stopped by that van parked in front of me
you looked at me, just as I looked at you
then you stepped towards my car
before stopping once again.

It was then, our eyes truly meet fully
connecting the final piece to the puzzle.
I know all too well who you are,
even beneath that face mask,

but all I could do was flash a smile to you
while shamefully blushing.

My eyes darted away from your gaze,
I was scared, shocked by this moment, this connection

but I could still see clearly out the corner of my eye
I was hoping it wasn't real, because I was scared
I'm still scared to know the truth, but I do
I can not escape the truth now
it was you, its always been you.

Your eyes never once moved away from me
they were like search lights that burned into me
forced upon me, that in itself shocked me
you stood there for far longer than you should,
and even now I still question why!

I know you were watching me all the while
but, I just remained silent, still and shocked
failing to hide within my car
I tried looking anywhere, but at you
yet, my eyes failed me,
because I kept you in my gaze,
like you kept me in your own
I couldn't help it, your truly beautiful.

I leaned slightly forward in my seat
fumbling with my sat-nav once more
you just remained stood there, near my car
making it all the more clear, you were truly there
this image, this time will haunt me till the day I die!

All the while you were observing me
just as much as I tried not to observe you
but all the same I was.

Do you know my whole world shattered then?

33

It was in that moment that our eyes met again
your mask was gone, and that smile you wore
it was bright, it sparkled within your eyes
just the thought of it now, months later,
brings tears to my eyes.

Did your eyes become lost in that gaze?
I know my eyes were lost upon you
I know you expected me to step from my car,
but how could I?

It was then I heard you speak
I heard your voice crystal clear
your voice, not a telepathic whisper
I saw your lips move, you said my name
that's all you said
you sounded as shocked as I felt
part of me wanted to run to you, wrap my arms around
you and cling to you
but other part of me wanted to hide
all I did was stay put in my car, filled with fear.

I still questioned if that encounter it was real
truth be told, I know it was real.

I mouthed your name in my shocked state
I know all too well that this time is sacred to you

your walks at this later hour are personal
they are between you and your fur baby
I would never wish to intrude.

That is why I never stepped out from my car

even if I had tried, my car door wouldn't open
I've kicked myself from never going to you that night
I've question that run round and around my mind
all the what ifs, but I know it was real,
that encounter is real
just like the spiritual connection we have.

Deep down I know we will meet again
this was just a chanced encounter
to let us both know we are indeed connected
that we are not insane.

Our paths shall cross again
but until that time
I know I'll be forever haunted by your smile
let alone your eyes.

Oh how cruel that accidental turn was
it led me there upon that street
shamefully fighting with my sat-nav.
Your icy blue gaze trapped my own eyes
that soft voice that rang out in the cool summer night air
its a memory, locked deep within my heart.

Purest Gemstone Eyes.

Your eyes, there is so much I could say about them
for eyes they are the purest of gemstones,
the purest of gateways, and your eyes?
Well they are my gateway drug
they shimmer in hues of blues and greens
shifting, swirling and switching in all their sparkle
that natural beauty that illuminates from your soul.

Your eyes light up with your warmest smile
let me watch them shift
from your rage to your joy.
For your eyes they can be black with rage,
sadness or sorrow
but they can also be the brightest blue
filled with happiness, love and passion.

Such power your eyes hold
in their natural aquamarine illumination
those hues of beauty, hues and shades of your soul
they shine so perfectly
that heart of yours deep within
for your eyes truly are my gateway drug.

Hundred Percent.

I won't lie, not to you
not after everything we've been though,
it's hit me pretty hard, that realization,
that I'm not insane.

Truly it is you, it has always been you
astralling to me, you lurking there in the shadows
in many ways I'm honoured,
yet, also shocked all the same.

This connection is truly real,
a hundred percent real
I know that now.

It took for one chance meeting,
however limited in contact,
to truly make me know, to make me aware
to truly make me listen and believe my gut feeling.

I take comfort in this small fact that it is you
I also know our paths will cross again,
my gut feeling tells me as much.

This situation is a slow and steady one
each stepping stone should be walked tenderly,

but feeling this connection so strongly
knowing a hundred percent it is truly real
like I thought, that alone in itself, is powerful.

I now truly know to believe in myself

to trust in myself, to trust my gut feeling,
in an odd reflection of the whole situation
I also know to trust in you, to believe in you as well.

Feeling this alone, knowing its real
oh my heart, my poor heart,
my fumbling fingers, fighting for the words to type
for my fingers are like the tears which fall
the unspoken words from my heart.

Tears of relief, amazement and utter love
but all the same they are happy tears,
just as they are sad for now I know, truly know,
but they are tears all the same
for it is a hundred percent real
that I'm not insane.

37

It's Time.

I need to drive, I need to get away from here
get out of the city, away from this encounter.
I'm not ready, yet all the same I am ready
I don't care what route I take to Brighton now,
just get me out of London,
get me away from this moment
away from this sacred place
now locked as a memory.

Round the roundabout,
down the slip road
continue along the motorway.
Still I ask myself, did that really happen?
Did I really lock eyes with him?
Did he truly mouth my name?
Was that truly him?

Yes, Yes it did happen, that really was him
we did truly lock eyes,
a magic moment that connected us
now magic that is far strong than before.

Is love magic? Is this feeling love?
Because love is what I saw in those eyes,
love is what I felt when I knew it was truly him

this spell that's been woven upon us for so long,
a spell which has bound us together
it's getting stronger now.
But still, it's not yet the time,
how cruel the hands of fate!

39

That fact alone is suffocating to me
and yet, I can still breath,
maybe I breath because that feeling?
Perhaps that feeling is what keeps me alive?

I needed to make the first move,
I know that now.
So the first services on my journey, I pulled over
I needed to reach out to you,
to start this new ball rolling
I set off that chain reaction
to get things moving forward for the future.

I was greeted by a ghostly midnight parking lot
it was safe, I knew I could make it happen.

I grabbed my phone
knowing I needed to send a polite message
explaining why I didn't get out of the car,
I knew you had expected it
we both knew who you are and who I am to you.

Yet I know those walks you take late at night
with your sweet dog, are a sacred time
I could not bring myself to disturb you
however much our eyes hungered for each other
for us to speak, I knew it was still not time.

But this brutal truth does not stop me reaching out
there are more ways to start this ball for the future
more ways to turn those mechanical clogs
so this message is my port of call, my final hope.

Hopefully you will read this digital message,
I'm even more hopefully you will reply,
but what am I saying?
I know you will reply, but when the time is right
because you and I both know the truth now,
that this connection is truly real.

But for now,
we stand on the home stretch of our true union,
of that I'm sure,
I've foreseen it in the pools of spiritual water
yet this time was to confirm what we did not believe.

I needed to make the next move,
so I'll kick the ball right back into your court,
just by sending you a message,
it's politely and respectfully, but now I'll wait,
and wait,
and wait a little more.

Brighton To Wales.

Back on the motorway
following that robotic voice
take the next junction,
stay on the left of the slip road,
take the second exit at the roundabout!
Fine, bark your robotic orders,
I'll ignore them all the same.

I know the route so well now,
I know the area where my friend lives.
I'll grab a quick coffee,
then rejoin the roar of the motorway
back round the M25, up to the M4
past Swindon, Bath and Bristol,
over the bridge into Wales.

I'm on the home stretch
round those country lanes,
up the hill, then down the road to park,
I home once again.

I'll clamber into bed, as the sun is rising
I'm tired now, the shock has finally set in,
yet Brighton to Wales is an easy journey
nothing much now to say,

just that I'm home, safe and sound.

Tired.

I'll set my alarm for eight thirty,
still my body wakes at seven.
Curse that insomnia,
curse that lack of sleep.

I feel like a zombie
it's as if I'm in a haze of drunken thoughts,
yet, no alcohol was consumed.
I'm just tired
my body refusing long hours of slumber,
maybe it's the fact I need to clean?

Out of bed I clamber
soft cotton cover my figure,
that faded pattern of my beloved PJ's,
down each step of the wooden staircase I tread,
a morning hunt for coffee.

The worktop beside the sink is covered
staked high with unclean pots and pans,
I really need to do the washing up
I also need to do the laundry,
but first coffee, this head needs help
for I'm a zombie in this lack of sleep.

Then my thoughts turn to the wonder of last night
my memory locked upon that glance of your eyes,
I feel my heart skipping a beat.
But somehow, I still turn to get the milk,
that moments going to haunt me

43

these thoughts, there forever etched on my mind
but still I know that I'm tired this morning
yet my house is a mess, and I need to clean
so I'll battle on cleaning
while my mind whirls with all the what ifs.

Hearts.

Last night was wonderful,
that poetry event was just an inspiration.
So much food for thought,
I'm so happy and glad I went.

I will thank the host once again
congratulate her on her success,
I want to find the other poets as well,
I would like to read their work in the future,
as it is, I would rather support other artists
than feel the suffocation of mainstream artists.

But I also need to explain to the host,
the full reason as to why I left early
hopefully she will understand,
after all she has a right to know.

So a quick message will do
giving her a quick look on the insanity that I live
she will understand it, I'm sure,
who knows, she might already know.
Yet a reply back is a line of hearts
truly she appreciates my thoughts
but clearly like me, she is tired too.

So Now, I Wait.

I will continue waiting,
the message is sent after all.
It sits waiting in that inbox, unread
it will seen soon enough,
I really don't need to worry.
I just need to wait,
for the sands of time are slipping
the ball is back in their court,
now its time to turn new clogs,
its time to sit and wait.

A Book In A Day.

The house is cleaned now
so what should I do?
I'm filled with inspiration to write,
maybe I should start another book?

Another collection of poetry, inspired of yesterday!
Yes, that's just it,
a collection inspired by one days adventure
a day filled with wonderment
let alone, excitement and the unexpected.

But I never expected to write this much
not by lunch time,
fifteen pages on, still inspiration flows.
This digital quill has taken over my life,
today it flows and flows
like the waves of never ending emotions,
never ending creativity.

It was time to pick up my digital quill once again,
so much had happened, I needed to write it up,
that intense encounter,
an odd moment of confirmation,
beauty of the unspoken,
that was my evening, it was filled with so much,

the emotions of wonder, inspiration and adventure.

Its all led me here, to this digital page,
each page being filled with 24 hours of emotions,
events which all happened at once

47

following one after another
like waves of the tide or a chain reaction.

I never expected to write a new book so quickly,
24 hours on from those events in London
with another 24 hours of sleepy haze,
but there upon that digital page with digital quill
is my work, my new collection,
my new book.

I need to take the time to edit
that too so quickly done,
it's amusing in some ways
a book complete in 48 hours,
I truly must have been inspired,
but will they every truly know
how much that night effecting me?

My Final Message To You.

This book is done, its complete
yet still, I feel I need to say thank you once again.

But my mind is focused upon him,
upon that chanced encounter,
that late Saturday evening in London
the city glow in a street that seemed abandoned
it will be forever etched upon my mind.

It is now Monday, the book is edited
I just need to put together a cover
one final look though
then I can plan to publish it.

So we've come to the end of this collection
inspired by one nights events,
a memory held sacred, locked away.
So many memories were made that night
but one will stand out above all,
those eyes of aquamarine, they will haunt me.

None the less, its time to live, and I shall
I won't shy away any longer
but I will also hold that look in my mind.

So on we walk in life, into the future we go
to all of you who read this,
all of you who bought this,
all of you who were gifted this,
thank you!

Not just for taking the time to read this
but for sharing and witnessing a memory,
a memory now locked within words.

49

About The Author.

Alixzandra F Wiseman is a self publishing author, mostly writing poetry and short stories. She has been writing poetry for the past three years and started self publishing her work as books in September 2021. Alixzandra is inspired by art and spirituality, she often believes that words are like the paint being written upon a canvas were the author is the artist creating a mental image for the reader, whether that image is felt by emotions or truly seen within the readers mind. Alixzandra writing is filled with a passion of the elements that are often misunderstood, a lot of her poetry and short stories work takes on the elements of romance and spirituality as if they are combined and over lapping, let alone her love for creatures of the night, such as vampires, witches and werewolves, she does use her own personal encounters within the spiritual and supernature world to inspire and create her written work.

Alixzandra started self publishing her work due to a heart-wrenching moment in her personal life. Being a single mother, on top of trying to find work and yet being discriminated against because of her personal situation, she turned her passion for writing into her career and has published a number of books in the last few months, with more books to come in the future.

If you are interested in seeing what Alixzandra is
working on for the future, and indeed what future books
are out for release, please check out her social media
pages.
Website:
https://lixwman.wixsite.com/zandrasparks

Her Personal Blog:
http://www.thewitchesboudoir.co.uk/

Facebook:
https://www.facebook.com/Ellaliljablackrosewriter

Twitter:
https://twitter.com/Alixzandraflo

Instagram:
https://www.instagram.com/alixzandraflo/?hl=en

Other Books By Alixzandra F Wiseman.

Picture The Mind – One Verse Poetry

Published September 2021
A collection of one verse poetry written to inspire the
mind, to view the world from another aspect of life, to
see details that would not always be seen.

Pleasure's Interlude.

Published November 2021
A short sexual romance story, written in point of view of
the reader to experience the love and heat of a
romantic interlude.

My Loving Astraller.

Published January 2022
A collection of romantic poetry inspired by an astral
traveller and romantic encounters within the astral
realms.

The Day Everything Changed.

Published March 2022
A collection of poetry inspired by events that happened
personally to Alixzandra F Wiseman in August 2021. A

mixture of life inspiration poetry as well as an odd
encounter that has since spun her world into a new
direction.

Upcoming Releases

Dream State.

Set for publishing July-August 2022
A short story written in point of view of the reader, a
story based on astral projection and spirituality, along
with a romantic encounter with a vampire emperor who
haunts the readers dreams, this vampire late comes to
find the reader physical in the world to free her from her
fear of insanity.

More to be announced at a later date of 2022.

All books are available as kindle books and paper back
books on Amazon and good reads.

www.ingramcontent.com/pod-product-compliance
Lightning Source LLC
Chambersburg PA
CBHW072127150726
47999CB00005B/2178